FREDGIE™

a CARNAVALESCO

FREDERICK L. KRAMER

To order additional copies of this book, contact:
Xlibris
844-714-8691
www.Xlibris.com
Orders@Xlibris.com

ISBN: Softcover   978-1-6641-9132-7
           Hardcover   978-1-6641-9131-0
           EBook   978-1-6641-9133-4

Print information available on the last page

Rev. date: 11/12/2021

DEDICATIONS:

To all the people who helped me grow artistically.

Beginning with Madeline Salow, who gave me my first class in Public Speaking when I was ten years old. Also, The American Mime Theatre, HB Studio, Alvin Ailey Dance Theatre. And to all the members of the Fredgie Show. Kate Lyra and Jintsy James.

Lastly, for my parents, who encouraged and supported me through the years.

CREDITS:

Linda J. Fazio, Melody Hillock, Eric Moser, Ronnie Goodrich, Zou Zou, Emily Russo, Claribel Diaz, Jean Phillipe and Dawn Gibson at Xlibris.

Tears of a Clown

"Fredgie is colorful and funny lik
Profound and pure like Cha
And as both of them,
Fredgie is a melancholic char

A poem by Martha Gonzales
(Personal Assistant to Fredgie)

FREDGI

In 1969,
entered
the age o
me these

Paul Cu
commitr
One pm.

E began in an unexpected Magical and Spiritual way.

while I was living in New York City and married with 2 young children, I
he American Mime Theatre to study this art form. Unbeknownst to me at
28 my world opened up to a whole new experience which has remained with
last 50 years.

tis was the Creator and Director of The American Mime Theatre. The work
ent was 4 days a week from six pm to nine pm and Saturday from ten am to
ou could not miss a class. This was my commitment for 4 years.

The American Mime Theatre, 1972. Fredgie on the far right, standing last row.

During this time, my name was Fred Kramer. The name Fredgie did not appear until 20 years later in 1988 while I was living in Brazil and the co-producer and on camera actor with The Kate Lyra Show. In Portuguese, (the "d" sound is pronounced like a "g", so Fred became Fredgie.) but in the meantime....

The workload at the American Mime Theatre, located in the East Village on 4th Street, had a specific curriculum. Basically, there was a combination of ballet, moving to words, and interpretation of dance movements. It was most important for us to learn to keep our bodies in alignment and learn to move to words without talking. This format became ingrained in our souls week after week to this very day. We had occasionally had performances, one of which was on the NBC's Today Show.

To keep my body in shape, I also joined the Alvin Ailey Dance Company. As well, I studied Theatre at The HB Studios with Bill Hickey. Also, I took up Fencing and Karate. For four years this was my life. In addition, I was an Art Dealer and selling Rolls Royce and Jaguar cars. I also wrote and published The White House Gardens book. In January of 1971, in New York City, my third son Oliver was born. But, in 1976 I was divorced and moved to New Hampshire to begin a whole new life with my children. For three years I managed the Maplehurst Inn in Antrim, New Hampshire.

Then we moved to Gregg Lake, just out of town. There I rented an old Victorian house and started making 5 pounds loaves of bread, called Mo's Mountain Bread. We would bake at night. Oftentimes, my logger friends would sit with me, drink their beers and play guitar while the bread was baking. We also made pizzas for everyone to enjoy. At five in the morning, we would load my van with 50 loaves of fresh smelling breads. The aroma was intense. I still remember the fragrant smell today. I delivered the bread to varies stores. One of the stores in Peterborough was owned by my dear friend Laurecy who had a cheese shop called My Whey.

She was my bread client for two years and I finally moved into her house with her two little girls.

We started a farm and had chickens. The girls would deliver eggs to our neighbors. Then we had sheep and pigs, rabbits and a goose. Everyone was busy eating. And I had lots of work to do. In addition, I had a beautiful vegetable garden and Laurecy did all the cooking with her excellent Brazilian recipes.

In August of 1987, while I was recovering from a skin cancer surgery at Brigham's & Women's Hospital in Boston, I looked at the mirror in my room and did not like the way my scars looked on my face from the recent plastic surgery. I didn't like the dull green colors on the hospital walls. I didn't want to return to the little farm where I was living in Peterborough, New Hampshire looking the way I did. I wanted a new purpose in life, but didn't know what it would be?

I prayed and asked for some guidance...All I saw in my visions were multi-colors... lots of colors...and I knew the world, at least my world needed to have bright colors to illuminate hope and sunshine instead of the drab green hospital walls and grey New England weather.

I told my doctor how upset I was with the new look of my face. He assured me that in time the scars would heal. (Little did I know at this time that in the future there would be many more surgeries and scars.)

But then, the doctor described how there were children far worse off than me in the Dana Farber Cancer Center and the Burn Unit down the street from my room. Their lives were to be shortened by their illnesses. The burn patients were permanently disfigured by their accidental wounds, many of them full body.

He told me how a little "make-up" could soften the look of my scars. The nurse showed me "before and after" photographs of a few burn patients.

I stopped feeling sorry for myself and in a flash, I knew I wanted to make people smile. After all, I always was the "class clown" when I was in school. So, why not do this again now- but how?

On the drive from Boston back to New Hampshire, I wondered how I could create my dream. All I knew was, that by thinking about others, I would stop thinking about myself...and so my new journey began.

6 year old Fredgie with Aunt Maxine and lil' cousin Hutch

In 1985 I had been studying Video Arts for 2 years at Keene State College, in Keene New Hampshire. It was 20 miles from my house and past famous Mount Monadnock. It means "the one who stands alone." At that time, the state of Video Arts was a half inch reel to reel system. The camera was very large and had only 15 minutes of a charged battery. It was cumbersome to manage, particularly compared to 30 years later in 2020 with the Apple 12 system. With which you can make a movie and a telephone call. But in 1987 a cell phone was yet to be developed. But coming soon.

During this time, I was making vignettes of local characters such as my dear friend Mad Dog Don Wright, a clarinet player who had been with the Ozzie Nelson Band years ago and was now retired and living in Peterborough, New Hampshire. Also, my friend Mo who was a lumberjack living in Antrim, New Hampshire. As well as several of his friends, such as Mush Cook who used to eat glass.

Mad Dog, Fred, and Blue Fish

Mad Dog at Mount Lemon, Tucson, AZ

Fredgie and friends, Peterborough, New Hampshire - 1997

In 1988, I traveled to Rio de Janeiro, Brazil with Laurcey to visit her father and to seek alternative therapies for my skin cancer. During my recovery, I became acquainted with Kate Lyra, a well-known Brazilian television personality. Together, we produced The Kate Lyra Show with Fredgie. Kate starred in this English language talk show. This was 1990 and we were the first cable Television show in Brazil. It was shot at the Copacabana Palace Golden Room Hotel Ballroom. We had many guests from English language schools in Rio and guests from the hotel. The show was in English and distributed in 4 and 5-star hotels in Rio. Through Kate's contact with American Express, we were able to get them to help sponsor our program.

As Fredgie, the vision for my life began to crystallize. I would dedicate my life to helping children interested in the arts start careers. When I was seven years old, there was no television, so I had no way to express myself except to clown around in school. Being a part of the Brazilian television world, it occurred to me what an amazing opportunity it would be if I could give theatrical kids a chance to appear on a television program.

In 1988, I won an award for a children's song I co-wrote, "Hippopotamus Rock" with Rosen Shontz and my work with children grew, as well as did my character. To understand my character development requires a brief lesson in the history of Brazilian television and a master showman, their national hero, Chacrinha. He hosted a musical variety show for kids in Brazil. He owned three bozinhas which are similar to a horn that he always used in the show. When he squeezed it, it would make a shrill blast. When Chacrinha died in 1988, one of his bozinhas was buried with him, one was put in a museum of Chacrinha in Sao Paulo, Brazil. The third was given to me by Terazinha Sodre, who starred in the show with Chacrinha. Terazinha was a co host of mine in my Miami Television show. She called me a carnavelsco, which means a showman in Portuguese, and so, I became Fredgie El Carnavelsco.

In 1991, I returned to the States and rejuvenated my Fredgie character through the help of a new friend, West Palm Beach TV personality, Jintsy James. She was a combination of Carol Channing and Phyllis Diller. I became producer and co-host of her show, Talk of the Town, which was a local and national produced TV show. My main function on the show as Fredgie was to interview various local talent.

Fredgie and Jintsy James

Fredgie and Jintsy James filming her show Talk of the Town, in Palm Beach, Florida

Fredgie arriving at the Jintsy James show – The Colony Hotel, Palm Beach, Fl

My clothing began to change as my character developed, leaning more towards a clownish attire. It was Jintsy's idea to take my character to the streets of Miami and see what kind of response I could get from the crowd. On a Saturday afternoon, in September, while walking about the people on South Beach and 10th Avenue, I met a gentleman selling hats which he had made. I bought one and it became my trademark. Developing a following lead to my own television show, The Fredgie Kids Show and the show Day Ninos. It was directed by Tom Wright from Los Angeles, who was living in West Palm Beach.

I decided to expand the venue and bring Salsa to Paris to attract an international audience. My solo act was staged along the walkway that fronts the Sacre Coeur Cathedral in Montmartre, in front of the Eiffel Tower, and at Place de Tertre. My attire included white tap shoes, baggy trousers, a red denim jacket, red clown nose, mirrored wrap around sunglasses and a psychedelic chimney sweep's hat. The act consisted of shaking a maraca and throwing it 30 feet in the air and catching it with my right hand. I would wiggle my hips and chant:

"Opa! Opa! Cha-cha-cha.

Mambo-and-merengue!"

To catch the audience off guard, I'd shuffle my feet and begin spinning in loopy pirouettes. My circles would grow erratic, until I would stumble or run into something, lose my equilibrium, and fall backward, landing on my derriere with my legs jackknifed in the air. Then, I'd brush myself off, do a little soft-shoe and tell my audience, "If you want to be a clown, the first thing you have to know is how to fall."

CANNES-MATIN
nice-matin

LE PREMIER QUOTIDIEN D'INFORMATIONS DU SUD-EST ET DE LA CORSE

MERCREDI 20 AVRIL 1994   SIÈGE SOCIAL : 214, route de Grenoble - 06290 NICE CEDEX 3 - Tél. 93.18.28.38

CANNES-MATIN, "The Premiere Daily Newspaper of Southeast France and Corsica":

MIP: FROM PALM BEACH TO LA CROISETTE
LAST ECHOS FOR FREDGIE, CLOWN-ENTREPRENEUR IN FLORIDA.   THE ULTIMATE INTERVIEW!

    For once, the last day will not have been the day the stands visibly
emptied and interviews were impossible. More active than ever, the arena
of television will have furnished just to the end it's share of drama.
For ourselves, in particular, thanks to our friend Fredgie. Never going
unnoticed in his starred-sequined-colored costume, greeting passers-by for
a few quick words, Fredrick Kramer hides beneath these trappings the
confirmed talent of a professional "distracteur". This member of The
American Mime Theater of New York is not only a street performer.
Surrounding him? The curious, of course, but also an entourage: Yes,
Fredgie is being televised. By satellite, to channels throughout
Latin America.

    Expressing himself in a melange of English-Spanish-Portugese to
which only he holds the key, Fredgie has won over even those in the
interior of the palace, where his tip-top presentation was the best
calling card for stealing a few moments from the busy scheduales of
those involved in the festival. And Fredgie, whose arrival we had
been noting for some time, couldn't keep himself from offering us
the microphone in order to present MIP. A short film sequence, a
cassette of which he has promised to send on to Cannes-Matin.
To be expected: this "professional tourist"-- it's written on his
calling card-- has his office and his connections in Palm Beach...
in Florida.   Champagne! Jean Philippe.

The television Academy show was in Cannes, France. I hired a TV cameraman and did my act and interviews as the people entered the Palais building. By chance, I met Jean Phillipe, who was a writer for the famous Nice-Matin newspaper. Needless to say, he "dug" my act.

I chanted "Shaka-shaka-shaka!" and encourage kids to join in the fun handing them my maracas and leading them into a dance. In the end, there would be great laughter and I'd ask, "Are you having fun with Fredgie?" Fredgie found his sense of mission frolicking with children in Paris. I had proven that children were attracted by the bright colors and noise and easily gravitated toward my character. I expanded my wardrobe to include dozens of bright, embroidered dinner jackets and, of course, many more of my new trademark, oversized colorful hats. All this time, I was very conscious of alignment and my dance form from my years studying at the American Mime Theatre and The Alvin Ailey Dance Company.

Fredgie at Cannes, France 1992

Back in the states, I expanded the act to include a talent Troupe and they appeared with me at various events, including visiting many children's hospitals. Troupe Members included: Mr. Silver who pretended to be a statue or did such acts as pulling scarves out of his mouth.

Fredgie with Mr. Silver

Zu-Zou, an acrobat and teacher, and Clowns; Latin Dancers including Luz La Rumba, a salsa dancer simulating Charo-esque maneuvers, Mr. Percussion, a fanciful drummer who will tap on anything; kids on roller skates, and child talent: Nayer Regalado (Fredgie's nine-year-old co-host), Claribel Diaz (a Vegas showgirl trapped in the body of a nine-year-old), Felix Reynoso (a Willie Chirino imitator), and Abraham Ascoy (a young Michael Jackson imitator.)

Fredgie with Paige the Clown

Fredgie with Tippy the Clown

Fredgie with Mr. Percussion

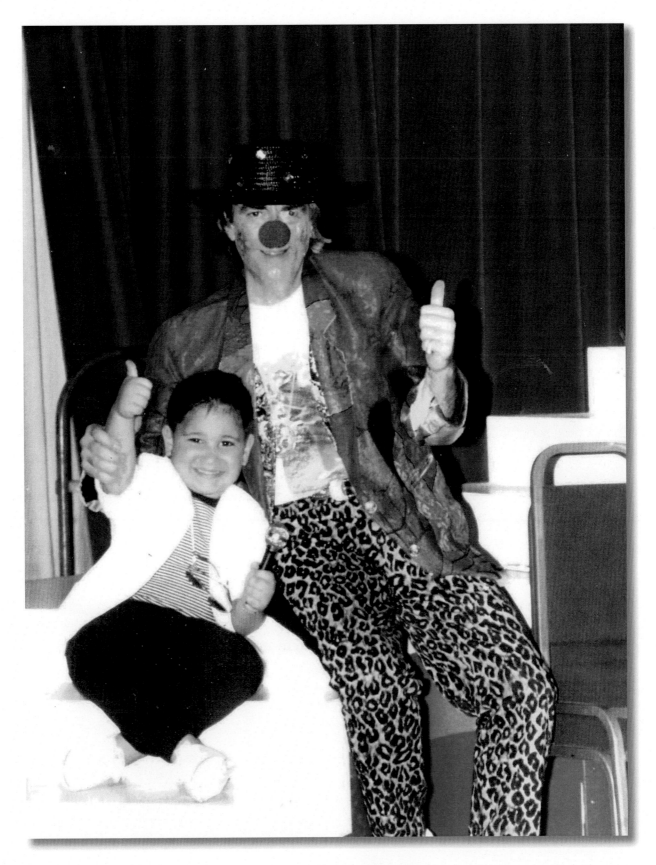

Fredgie with Felix Reynoso

Fredgie dancing with Luz La Rumba

To be a success, I knew marketing was key. I developed a Fredgie press kit which included Fredgie pennants, buttons, necklaces, plastic cups, squeeze bottles, T-shirts, autograph pads, nerf balls, beach balls, shoelaces, pom poms, maracas, and a Fredgie Corn-E-Fono (you fill it with popcorn and then pop out the bottom and it becomes a megaphone). These and copies of my performances were given away as promotional gifts.

Nearly every public appearance I made was preserved on video-tape, ultimately compiling enough material for over 26 television episodes. Some were filmed in Scala, a Brazilian restaurant and night club in Miami, Florida. Others were filmed at various events: the Three Kings' Day Parade, a trade event in Coconut Grove, the Grand Marshall for the Candy Cane Parade in Hollywood, Florida, etc.

Fredgie El Maximo's International All Star Latin Music Dance Festival aired on Saturday mornings at 9:30 on various channels in Miami and the Gold Coast, such as Ole TV in Little Havana, Brazilian TV, Adelphia, as well as, we were on a television station in Los Angeles, CA at KMET-TV and also aired on a television station from Honduras. I also organized Fredgie Workshops which specialized in Yoga, Mime, Watercolor, and "Temple Dance."

TELEVISION

2 September 1994

Mr. Fred (Fredgie) Kramer
Jack Yukon Productions

Via Fax (305) 789-2999 #1668

To my Good Friend Fredgie:

     Congratulations on you wonderful new children's program.
The local response here in Los Angeles is wonderful. You have
paved the way for a whole new entertainment package. I am
looking forward to the many episodes ahead.

     Your local affiliate in Hollywood wishes you the best.

Sincerely,

Charles Lohr
General Manager

KMET-TV 38

6611 Santa Monica Blvd.

Los Angeles, California

90038-1311

Tel.   213.469.5638

Fax.   213.469.2193

All of this work allowed me to be nominated and become a member of the Television Academy of Arts and Sciences, Los Angeles and a member of the famous FRIARS Club in Beverly Hills, California.

My friend and Publicist, Mike Conley, sponsored me to the Television Academy, which votes on the Emmy Awards. My peer group was Children's Programing. Additionally, I attended many of the offerings for new films which were shown in the Great Hall.

At the FRIARS Club, during the time I was a member, I met many of the old guard, such as, Steve Allen, Larry King, Milton Berle, Red Buttons, Ron Northey, Jack Carter, Jan Murray, and many others. One of my favorite moments was attending Milton Berle's 90th birthday party at the Beverly Hills Hotel. When Jan Murray, the emcee asked Miltie what he wanted for his 90th birthday, Uncle Miltie answered without hesitation "91!"

My famous Uncle Miltie story is that when I was 13 years old and trying out for football, it was determined that I had a hernia that needed to be removed from my right groin. At the Barnert Hospital in Paterson, New Jersey, in 1954, I stayed for three days. On the second day the nurse came into my room and said "you know who is next door, Uncle Miltie. I am going to go next door to see if he will come in to see you." I couldn't believe I would meet the famous Milton Berle who had his television show. Every Sunday at brunch, I would imitate his show from Saturday night to my parents.

A few minutes later, into my room walked Uncle Miltie. Years later I found out he was there visiting his mother-in-law, who lives in Paterson, New Jersey.

The nurse said, "don't make him laugh, he has new stitches." Uncle Miltie came over to me and said, "How ya doin' kid?" and then he pinched my cheek. And then he put his two hands on his ears and stuck his tongue out at me. He made me laugh. He turned, and as he left the room, he pinched my right foot. I always remembered this moment. It was almost forty years later when I had lunch at the FRIARS Club with my friend Bob Kessel, he told me that Milton Berle was having lunch at "his" table in the corner. Bob knew my story and told me to go tell Uncle Miltie but be ready for a lot of "heckling".

So, up I stood and walked over to "his" table, he was eating lunch with a few other people, I piped in, "Hello Uncle Miltie, I am a new member here and I have a story to tell you when I met you when I was 13 years old in the Barnert Hospital in Paterson,

New Jersey." After telling him my story, he told me that before television, he used to work at a theatre in Paterson, New Jersey, five shows a day, six days a week for $125.00. He asked me if I knew the name of the theater. I said no but my mother might. So, I went to the public telephone and called my mother in Passaic, New Jersey, and I asked her. I told her I was with Milton Berle. This was 1994 and cell phones were not used yet. She told me it was the Fabian Theater. I rushed back to "his" table and told Uncle Miltie. He said "Yes, the Fabian!" Then he said, "Sit down kid and let's talk!"

Fredgie holding bozinhas

Fredgie at the FRIARS Club with "Charlie Chaplin"

April 10, 2021

"VIVA FREDGIE ! Little did I realize the day that I was referred by Gary Freedline of Video Keepsakes to interview "Fredgie, A Clown About Town" that my life would be influenced to the point of changing it's destiny entirely. I was so impressed by all of the dreams that Fred Kramer "Fredgie" had accomplished for himself and others. He was so charming and spoke of so many interesting places that he traveled to and performed in the world. It was then that I suddenly proposed to him that he hire me and that together we could produce a Children's TV show that would not only promote his talents but would also publicize all of the International talents of children and adults that Fredgie would discover through auditions with a professional judge's panel. The Fredgie International Children's TV Show could in turn travel all over the world as Fredgie had always done before; except from then on he would travel with a joyous elenco creating fabulous memories for all! [Public & Cast) Guess What?? He did hire me and my fascinating life with that meaningful character of Fredgie began!

VIVA FREDGIE! LONG LIVE FREDGIE AND HIS FABULOUS CHARACTER CREATING UNITY OF THE RACES THROUGHOUT THE ENTERTAIMENT INDUSTRY!!

- Ronnie Goodrich

Ronnie Goodrich was my Producer and Talent Coordinator. She coordinated all the acts that appeared. Without her, the show could not go on. Gary Freedline was the Camera Production Company and Film Editor. Without his wizardry, the show could not be produced.

Fredgie with Carlos Oliva at Calle Ocho, Miami, FL

When I think back to the days when we had the Fredgie Show, a big smile crosses my face. I remember getting up every day and thinking "I love my job" while driving to work with the show. It was a magical time, working with Fredgie, the amazing adult team and all the talented kids. Personally, it was my dream job. As co-producer I got to be creative in so many ways, from choreographing, sitting in editing sessions, rehearsing with the kids, performing, shopping for costumes, and creating characters with Fredgie. We were so blessed to have had this joyful time together, to perform live and also broadcast the show on TV for everyone to enjoy. Thank you Fredgie for this wonderful slice in time.

Zou Zou

Fredgie with Martha Gonzales and Zou-Zou (far right)

Zou Zou, Carl and Fredgie

Miami NewTimes

The SURFIES

July 21 – 27, 1994

By Steven Almond

**Hollywood has the Oscars. Broadway has the Tonys.
The time has come to honor local teevee with its very own award.**

The irrepressible Fredge (love that hairstyle)

Fredgie-osity
And the Surfie goes to...
*Fredgie's International
El Maximo All-Star Latin
Music Dance Festival*

Trying to describe Fredgie to those who haven't seen him is a little like trying to describe a rainbow to the colorblind. Or an acid trip to a monk. Fredgie is basically an insane person from New Jersey who spent some time in Brazil and returned wearing psychedelic clothing and saying "¡Oye! ¡Oye!" a lot. He interviews members of the Latin glitterati, mostly at local clubs, though never in any recognizable language. There is no structure, per se, to the show.

La Scala, Miami, Florida

Fredgie Performing at La Scala, Miami, Fl

Fredgie at Candy Cane Parade, Hollywood, Florida

Fredgie at the Jackie Gleason Theater, Miami, Fl - 1992

Claribel Diaz – Dancer and Child Fashion model.

My name is Claribel Diaz, when I auditioned for The Fredgie Kids Show I was just barely eight years old. A skinny, cute, over-active hip little dancer ready to take on the world!

I was fascinated to be chosen by the judge's panel. Therefore, giving me the opportunity to display my talent with Fredgie on the Kids Show where I could compete with children of all nation's with Fredgie, The Clown, a Carnavalesco - Showman, Master of Culture and the Arts; as our Chief Director.

I have so many memories of traveling with Fredgie and my friends to different cities and countries to perform.

Parent scouts would also accompany us, as Fredgie was very strict with all of us. He not only taught us to perform and act but also to be responsible for our actions. All of the children wanted to pose in front of the camera next to Fredgie so that all of their friends could see them on Saturday morning.

I was very lucky, as I became one of the most popular dancers on the Fredgie Kids Show in turn giving me the opportunity to make my own salary and help my mother and father to buy my special attire and accessories that I would wear when we would attend special coming out parties for the different TV segments.

Thank you Fredgie for giving me my big break! I also won different dance contests at the time on Univision Latin Channel on the Don Francisco Show.

Fredgie was not a selfish producer as he gave the children on his show the rights to appear on other popular TV shows. Also, making him very popular with young performers.

Fredgie with Claribel
Fredgie received many awards such as The Film Advisory Board Award and
the Flamingo Award for the best new television show in Florida.

Fredgie receiving The Film Advisory Board Award from Ann Blythe, Hollywood, California

Fredgie also traveled to varies conferences such as the NATPE - The National Association of Television Producers and Executives in Las Vegas, Nevada and Cannes, France. He met the famous XuXa from Brazil at the Las Vegas show.

Fredgie with XuXa. Las Vegas, Nevada, 1990 at NATPE

Fredgie at Days Inn, Miami Beach, Florida

Fredgie was in Mexico City filming with Azteca TV, 1991.

Fredgie at Temple of the Sun, Mexico City, 1991

The following storyboard was designed to become a comic book feature. It was designed by Stone Soup, Dallas, Texas.

Here Comes Fredgie

Story Board Book

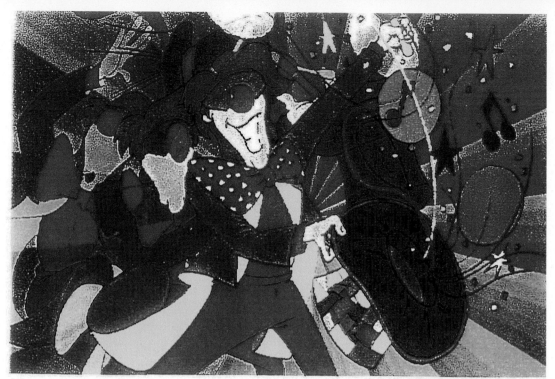

His arms are outstretched, fumbling for the hat with one hand and his maraca with the other.

Sus brazos estan extendidos, busca su sombrero con una mano, y su [maraca] con le otra.

The hat erupts with balloons, confetti, birds, flowers, toys, etc.

El sombrero se explota con globos, confetti, pájaros, flores, juguetes, excetera.

As confetti blasts out of the bottom, it carries him up into the air.

El confetti se explota fuera del fondo, lo lleva hacia arriba en el aire

He waves and goes into orbit with "Here comes Fredgie" following behind him. The children yell, OPA! EPA! WOW! as the words appear at the bottom of the title screen.

El saluda y va en órbita con "Aquí viene Fredgie, siguiendo lo. Los niños gritan, ¡OPA! ¡EPA! ¡WOW! sequn las palabras aparecen en el televisor.

Pose Number 5

It's a figure stumbling towards the screen. Beat continues. Figure resolves into Fredgie.

La Figura tropieza hacia la pantalla. Golpea, continuamente. La Figura se convierte en Fredgie.

The bottom of Fredgie's basket open up. A hook on a rope is lowered. We see the hook grab the villain's coat collar. He tries to fight it but can't reach behind him. FREDGIE snaps his fingers.

El fondo del cesto de Fredgie se abre hacia arriba. Se baja un gancho en una soga. Vemos el gancho agarra el cuello de la chaqueta del ladron. Trata de luchar, pero él no puede alcansar detrás él. FREDGIE shena sus [cliquea] dedos.

EACH OF HIS TROUPE's instruments become pinata sticks. They beat the living %$@! out of him. The stuff he stole begins to fall out.

CADA UNO DE los instrumentos de SU Compañia se vuelven palitos de [piñatas]. Le pegan sin compassion %$@! fuera de él. El material que robó, empieza a caer fuera.

From a low angle, Fredgie rise up into the sky. He leans out and gives Mr. Percussion the high sign. MR. PERCUSSION, JOJO SPARKLES, LUZ LA RHUMBA, TIPPY THE CLOWN, ZOU-ZU and the children NAYER LA REINA, CLARIBEL and FELIX begin to form the conga line.

De un bajo ángulo Fredgie sube hacia arriba al cielo. Se apoya afuera del globo y le da La Señal Alta A El Señor Percusión. Señor PERCUSION, JOJO CHISPEA, LUZ LA RHUMBA, EL PAYASO TIPPY, ZOU-ZU y los niños NAYER "LA REINA", CLARIBEL y FELIX empiesan a form ar una línea de conga.

The villain tries to escape to the right, he's bumped back to the left by someone's hips. He's bumped again. Pinball sounds are made with each bump. As he falls to the ground. His eyes read "TILT."

El bandido trata de escapar a la derecha, se golpea por las caderas de alquin, lo tiran izquierdo hacia la izquierda. Se golpea de nuevo. El sonido del pinball sique con cada choque. Se cai al piso y sus ojas expresan la palabra "TILT".

A wider shot shows a woman wearing a mau-mau and an apron. Her hands reach in carefully to remove the pie from the oven, her hands are scorched by the intense heat of the tray. She screams -WOMAN-AAiiyyeeeee!! She throws the pie up into the air.

En una tira más ancho muestra una mujer sobre peso, de piel osoura vestida con un [mau-mau] y un delantal. Sus manos alargan en cuidadosamente shcan el pastel del horno, sus manos son quemadas por el intenso calor de la bandeja. ¡Grita- MUJER-AAiiyyeeeee!! Tira el pastel hacia arriba al aiqre.

Her HUSBAND sits at the kitchen table, forked poised ready to eat, salivating. He tries to bite the pie as she walks by him. He bites the aroma, leaving his teeth marks in it.

Su MARIDO se sienta en la mesa de la cocina, su tenedor balanciadó listo para comer, se savorea. Trata de morder él pastel cuando élla camina por al lado de él. Muerde el aroma, quedan sus dientes marcado en él.

He quickly grabs the pie before falling to the ground. He tips his hat - CHA-CHING - to the lady as if to say "Thank You." As she waves her fist at the villain, screaming.

Rápidamente agarra el pastel ante gue se caiqa a la tierra. Ladea su sombrero- CHA-CHING- a la dama como diciendole "muchas gracias." ELLA le apunta su puño gritando "bandido".

FREDGIE removes his hat and sets it upside down on the ground. A magic balloon begins to rise from inside. It is becoming a hot air balloon.

FREDGIE se quita su sombrero y lo coloca arebes en la tierra. Un globo mágico empieza a subir de adentro. Se vuelve un globo caliente aéreo.

My spiritualist - Gabrielle

Fredgie with Nayer at her 10th birthday party, Miami, Florida

Fredgie with Nayer

 **THE MOST IMPORTANT EVENT OF THE XXI CENTURY...!**

A Feature Film

Paulo Gulano, the band leader with Fredgie, Mr. Percussion and Martha Gonzales

Fredgie! Opa, Opa!

My life has been totally changed by observing the many gifts and talents of this generous man. He was the image of my "Daddy Warbucks" that kind man you went for advice, was touched by his love and understanding, and was nurtured beyond all expectations.

Fredgie gave you the view of his magical, happy world and made you a part of it. There was always joy, laughter, song and dance; the mingling of all colors displayed like never before! He did it all and we loved being a part of the magic.

As Fredgie would say, "Find your stage and shine!" Opa, Opa!

And we did! Heads above the rest!

Gracias,

Love, Jo Jo Sparkles

Fredgie and Jo Jo Sparkles with Children

Fredgie with Jo Jo Sparkles and Tommy

Fredgie with Jo Jo Sparkles and singer Mark Anthony

All in all, The Fredgie Show came and went with the 1990's. It was ahead of it's time.

Hand drawn caricature of Fredgie-Cannes, France

Hand drawn caricature of Fredgie-Cannes, France

Lillia La La Magnifica

Fredgie performing at La Scala, Miami, FL

Fredgie – The Executive Producer

Printed in the United States
by Baker & Taylor Publisher Services